Hers

Hers

Maria Laina

Translated from the Greek by
Karen Van Dyck

WORLD POETRY BOOKS

This book is made possible with support from
the Stavros Niarchos Foundation.

First Edition, First Printing, 2022
ISBN 978-1-954218-00-0

World Poetry Books

New York City, NY / Storrs, CT
www.worldpoetrybooks.com

Distributed by SPD/Small Press Distribution
Berkeley, CA
www.spdbooks.org

Library of Congress Control Number: 2022931247

Cover design by Dalia Karpaviciute
Typesetting by Ainee Jeong & Don't Look Now
Printed in the USA by McNaughton & Gunn

Contents

The Place of the Page:
Translating Maria Laina's *Hers*

My translation of Maria Laina's *Hers* (*Δικό της*, 1985) originally appeared in *The Rehearsal of Misunderstanding*, a bilingual anthology of three collections by Greek women poets published by Wesleyan University Press in 1998. The aim of the anthology was to introduce readers in the United States to a new style of elliptical poetry written in the wake of the Dictatorship (1967–1974) by women who had grown up under the colonels' censorship. In the hands of these women, the use of cinematographic sequences of images formerly employed to evade the censors became a feminist strategy for undermining patriarchy. *Hers* was a search for a place where her story could spread out over pages and take up the space it needed. It was a pivotal piece that teased out the relation between censorship, gender, and poetry in Greece.

I remember meeting the poet in the late 1980s at her apartment on Tydeos Street in Athens. I had brought a list of questions for her to answer. What struck me then and sticks with me to this day was her lack of interest in my being there. An accomplished translator herself, she valued translation. But why this need to meet? Surely my translation was my business. To me her blank stare came right out of the pages of *Hers*—the same quiet insularity, the same unwillingness to express expectation or to believe in an audience—but it took me many years to understand the implications that this attitude carried for translation. She wasn't simply trying to numb pain, to disengage. No, she was also expressing her conception of translation, the idea that it belonged more to the receiving language and culture than to those where the source text originated. As a translator, I had to make the decisions. She couldn't make them for me. The visit helped me understand my responsibility as a translator as well as her poetry.

From early collections like *Change of Place* (*Αλλαγή τοπίου*, 1972) and *Punctuation Marks* (*Σημεία στίξεως*, 1979) up to the present, the central problem in Laina's poetry has been how to accept a gaze that censors by means of neglect, how to talk about a kind of love that others can't recognize. At times ascetic, at others autoerotic, the love described is rarely reciprocal, never heterosexual, and most often at odds with societal norms. Invoking Sappho's fragmentary women-centered past and Cavafy's imagined homoerotic future ("Someday in a more perfect society..."), *Hers* sets itself the task of making room for her kind of love, in the absence of any support. As Maria, the main protagonist, states:

> besides in this narrative
> the difficulty
> of finding a space is clear

In choosing the name Maria for her protagonist, Laina draws on a long tradition of writers who have tried to pin down the role of women in Greek society. Maria, the most common of Greek female names, is both the holiest of mothers and the most profligate of whores, the Virgin Mary and Mary Magdalene, and the namesake of the poetry collection *Maria Nefele* by the Nobel Laureate Odysseas Elytis. Maria is also, most importantly, the author's own name. *Hers* critiques attempts to keep women intact and in place, subordinate and heterosexual, offering instead an alternative discourse that is not monumentalizing and totalizing. If representation is fundamentally an untrustworthy process, Laina's poetry will display this uncertainty through a poetics of evasion. As the epigraph warns: "In everything she did she sought herself; no one should trust her." Rather than trying to salvage an ideal or a whole, the collection flaunts disaggregation. Censorship and claustrophobia are seen to be not only restrictive and disabling, but also productive of a new minimalist language and way of being.

The first poem of the collection, "Wall Painting," imitates an archaeological report that attempts to excavate a woman in a crumbling Minoan fresco:

> The beginning of the thighs still remains
> a dull blue
> to the left a section of foot unadorned
> and a section from the hem of the dress.

The poem continues in this dry descriptive vein: "Most of the lower part / of the face is missing." The final line, however, is set off typographically, initiating a more conversational tone that characterizes the rest of the collection and states the real problem: "the ground of love is missing." The implied archaeologist is looking for the wrong thing. Even if it were possible to put the woman back together again, certain parts would still be missing— the mouth, for example, so important for speech and love.

In the ensuing collection Maria proceeds to give us snapshots of what it would mean to exist in pieces as well as in flux, outside of patriarchy's status quo. Except for the longer introductory poem and a prose epilogue, the book is composed of 59 very short fragments, each relaying a gesture, a thought, or a memory. These bits and pieces are divided into eight sections, each of which begins with Maria in the process of representing herself or being represented: in a mirror, in a votive offering, in a photograph. Laina draws our attention not to what is being represented but to the set-up that enables it: the position of Maria in front of the mirror, the kind of stone in which the relief is carved, the act of developing the photograph. And these initial poems of each section all contain some gesture or word that suggests that it will not be an easy mimetic relationship—fidgeting, fixing, rearranging, surprise, or discomfort is always present. The Lacanian lesson of subjective coherence as misrecognition seems to be the starting point. What Maria sees in the mirror never exactly matches who she is, and this complicated relationship must be repeatedly rehearsed. Like an unmarked box of memorabilia that tells a life story in no particular order, these poems invite us to shuffle through all the different ways identification is interrupted. They leave Maria alone, inhering less in the words than in the white space, in their interstices, not knowing anything for certain. As the epilogue concludes: "And me, what do I know? What do I know?"

The fragmented discourse of self in *Hers* produces a palimpsest of shifting perspectives that establishes the page as the place where Maria can be as she is, in pieces and more than one thing at one time. The frequent omission of pronouns, the confusion between the active and passive voice of verbs—these features intensify the need for a *topos* that can deal with surreal contradictions. In the Greek the same phrase can be translated "the body that remembered" or "the body she remembered," "she dreamt a golden deer lay down" or "she dreamt herself laying down a golden deer," "her name was invoked" or "she invoked her name." When pronouns do appear, they tend to slip around without any explanation. The "She" suddenly becomes "I":

> She does not participate
> I read, however, and

A "him" is introduced only to vanish.

Reading is not only something Maria does. At times it actually determines how we understand her relation to the world. In one poem Maria looking into the mirror is compared to the position of two words:

> The past scrubbed with water and ashes.
> Maria laughs
> Turns and takes her place again.
>
> Jasper and jasmine opposed.

As in English the place where ἴασπις κι ὁ ἴασμος ("jasper and jasmine") face each other in Greek is on the page of the dictionary. It is the reader who must establish a typographic relation between Maria and her reflection. And again, the reflection is not perfect. The words share the first three letters, but then, in both the Greek and in my translation, the equation breaks down. Complete correspondence is foiled.

In another poem the word that clues us in to the impossible reflection is "anathematic," an adjective used by archaeologists to describe a votive inscription or visual depiction of a tribute. Like the fresco and the mirror, the object described in this poem is meant for the viewer and, as usual, the reflection is skewed, "unnatural":

> There is no doubt.
> Both the orientation

and the inclination
(frontal and unnatural)
prove it.
Stone, of course
anathematic

The unnaturalness also has something to do with love. The Greek nouns "κατεύθυνση" and "προορισμός," in my translation "orientation" and "inclination," also refer to sexual preference. The adjective "unnatural" recalls other adjectives that were used to describe her body in preceding poems: "indifferent," "awkward," or more literally "uncoordinated." The Greek alpha-privative that turns words into their opposites (like the English prefix "un") infuses this series. Nothing is as it is meant to be.

In another fragment, a vase is the "πρόθεση" or "intention" of flowers—since, when it is empty, its presence suggests the flowers that are not there—but it also positions the flowers, controlling the placement of things like a "preposition," the other sense of the Greek word. Discourse, like desire, is a way of holding things together, but *her* discourse, like *her* desire, is different, disjointed:

She even dragged with her
the birds from the rug
and then she left
without elbows
or knees.

References to other literary works, from Shakespeare to modern Greek poetry, are everywhere in the collection. The vexed issue of finding room is clearer if we recall another "Maria" poem by Miltos Sachtouris, a surrealist poet of the post-WWII generation who greatly influenced the poets of Laina's generation through his visual vocabulary and plain language. While Sachtouris's "Maria" is a single page, Laina's fills a whole collection. While his Maria is still trapped within the traditional four walls of the domestic sphere, Laina's takes off, flies away, drifts into the space of other pages. The poetry of Cavafy also comes into play, not only as a utopian signpost for a more perfect society, but in the use of typography to create a space for such desire. In his poem "In the Same Space," which Laina refers to, Cavafy describes how love is demarcated by the locations where desire is felt—in the café, the bedroom, the taverna—but also by the page where desire is manifested through line and stanza breaks as well as spelling. Another important link is across media, to Peter Handke's film *The Left-Handed Woman*, which offers Laina a way to make Maria appear to be "staring out," frame after frame. Like Handke's protagonist, Maria doesn't fit in and has trouble communicating with others. There is no attempt to socialize the misfit as the traditional bildungsroman would. Instead, the collection, like the film, provides a place where the reader must acknowledge her, and the language in which she discovers herself, as her own.

At times this collection suggests that Maria's escape to this other place dates back centuries—to an ancient matriarchy in the period of the fresco, before metal and cotton. At other times, it is still to come, in the future, when the soft stone has crumbled and writing has been wiped away. More than anything, though, *Hers* insists, it is a place right now, right here, "out in the light," in the book we, her readers, are holding.

❦

So why republish this collection now? One reason is that it never had its own audience, since it came out with two other collections as part of a larger argument about contemporary Greek women's poetry. The translation needed space to speak for itself without the other collections. Also, it seemed to me that its minimalist feminist poetics might have more traction now in the US after L=A=N=G=U=A=G=E, the ensuing elliptical turn that included such women poets as Matthea Harvey, Susan Wheeler, and C.D. Wright, and translations like Anne Carson's *If Not, Winter: Fragments of Sappho*. But perhaps the most important reason was my sense that in this faster, busier millennium we might all profit from spending time in the quiet, interstitial space of *Hers*. It is a book that teaches us to slow down and wait.

In preparing this new edition I was concerned whether the interpretation I had developed regarding the narrative power of the fragment and its palimpsestic ability to accrue meaning over time and space was still served by my translation given how language and poetic contexts change. To this end I made a few changes. The title of the first poem "Fresco" became "Wall Painting," for example, to stress the way writing functioned in room after room and poem after poem. I also wanted to point readers to Laina's many references to painting: not just the Minoan frescoes from Knossos, but also more contemporary works with abstract representations of women by artists such as Miró and Rousseau. I made the sexual politics of the votive poem more visible by using not only the word "inclination" for "προορισμός," but also the word "orientation," instead of "direction," for "κατεύθυνση." I was curious whether the translations of the poems by Sappho and Cavafy, which I felt were driving *Hers*, were available to my readers in English. I recalled the H.D.-inflected translations of Sappho's fragments by Mary Barnard, her "I love that / which caresses / me" with my "I caress my body / I caress my awkward body." In this revision I also made the Cavafy intertext more noticeable by changing "in the same area" to "in the same space," the title most translators of Cavafy have given the poem in English (Keeley and Sherrard, Mendelsohn).

I wondered if at times my translation undid some of the ambiguities in the source text: my choice, for example, to use the more active sense of verbs in places when both an active and a passive meaning were possible in the

Greek. Should I sometimes choose the more passive sense? But then I began to notice another elliptical sensibility I had created through suspended syntax: "because she dreamt herself lying down / a golden deer in the valley." If the first kind was only possible in Greek, where pronouns aren't necessary, this kind was inherently English, where word order, not case, determines who is doing what to whom, so I left it as it was. But when I noticed a word had changed meaning since the 1980s and 1990s, I did feel compelled to find a new one. The adverb "totally," for example, had become a slang way to bide time, like "um." "Completely" was more appropriate to the Zen minimalism I was trying to create. These were small changes, but important ones. Translations need updating.

Karen Van Dyck, August 2021, Syros

Δικό της

Hers

Σ᾽ ὅλες τίς πράξεις γύρευε τόν ἑαυτό της·
κανείς δέν πρέπει νά τῆς ἔχει ἐμπιστοσύνη.

In everything she did she sought herself;
no one should trust her.

Τοιχογραφία

Σώζεται ἡ ἀρχὴ ἀπ' τοὺς μηρούς
σὲ ἄτονο γαλάζιο
τμῆμα ποδιοῦ ἀκόσμητο πρὸς τὰ ἀριστερὰ
καὶ τμῆμα ἀπολήξεως φορέματος.
Στὸ δέρμα διακρίνονται γραμμὲς
κυρίως ὀξυκόρυφες.
Ὁ χῶρος τοῦ λαιμοῦ διακόπτεται
ἀπ' τὸν ἀριστερὸ βραχίονα
ποὺ φέρεται πρὸς τὰ ἐπάνω
ἐνῶ μονάχα τὸ δεξὶ στῆθος δηλώνεται
μὲ ἐλαφρὰ καμπύλωση.
Ἀπὸ τὸ κάτω μέρος τοῦ προσώπου
λείπει τὸ μεγαλύτερο κομμάτι.
Κόκκινα τρίγωνα ἢ τόξα
σ' ὅλο τὸ ἄσπρο τοῦ βολβοῦ.
Σώζεται ἐπίσης ἡ κορδέλα τῶν μαλλιῶν
καὶ ἡ στροφὴ τοῦ σώματος
ποὺ ἀσφαλῶς προϋποθέτει
ἀνάλογες κινήσεις τῶν χεριῶν.

Λείπει τὸ ἔδαφος τοῦ ἔρωτα.

Wall Painting

The beginning of the thighs remains
a dull blue
to the left a section of foot unadorned
and a section from the hem of the dress.
On the skin lines are visible
mainly sharp angles.
The neck area is interrupted
by the left arm
which is raised up
while only the right breast is registered
by a slight curve.
Most of the lower part
of the face is missing.
Red triangles or arcs
cover the white of the eye.
The hair ribbon also remains
and the body's twist
which surely presupposes
similar movements in the hands.

The ground of love is missing.

1

Ἡ Μαρία μέσα στὸν καθρέφτη
ὁλόσωμη
στρώνει τὸ φόρεμά της στὸ λαιμό.

Δὲν ἔχει σημασία τώρα ποῦ ξαπλώνει τὸ κορμί της
ἂν ἔγινε σημύδα ἢ χορτάρι
ἡ Μαρία μέσα στὸν καθρέφτη
στρώνει τὸ φόρεμά της στὸ λαιμό.

Maria in the mirror
full-length
straightens her dress at the neck.
It does not matter now where her body lies
whether she turned to birch or grass
Maria in the mirror
straightens her dress at the neck.

Τριμμένο μὲ νερὸ καὶ στάχτη παρελθόν.
Ἡ Μαρία γελάει
γυρίζει καί ξαναπαίρνει τὴ θέση της.

Ἀντικριστὰ ὁ ἴασπις κι ὁ ἴασμος

The past scrubbed with water and ashes.
Maria laughs
turns and takes her place again.

Jasper and jasmine opposed

Δὲν εἶναι ἐδῶ
οὔτε ἄλλοτε·
ἄλλοτε ἦταν.
Ὁ ἔρωτας εἶναι ἀλλοῦ
καὶ μόνη της
δὲν ἦταν ποτέ.

She is not here
nor was she;
once she was.
Love is elsewhere
and never
was she alone.

Ἡ Μαρία στέκεται
σωπαίνει ἀμίλητη.

Ὡραῖο φῶς τῆς μέρας.

Maria stands
grows silent.

Fair daylight.

Ἡ ὕπαρξη στὸν ἴδιο χῶρο
δύο ὁλόβαφων τριγώνων
καὶ δίπλα τους νὰ διακρίνεται ἡ ἀρχὴ
κίτρινου χρώματος
τὴν ἄφηνε ἀδιάφορη·
ἀφοῦ καὶ νὰ μισεῖ μποροῦσε
κατὰ τὸν ἴδιο τρόπο ποὺ ἀφοσιώνεται στὸ κέντημα.

The existence in the same space
of two solid color triangles
and next to them the beginning
of a yellow color
left her indifferent;
since she could also hate
the same way she devoted herself to needlework.

Καθὼς μεγαλώνει
ἀναχωρεῖ μὲ περισσότερη ἄνεση.

Ἴσως καὶ κάποια ἕλξη.

As she grows older
she departs with greater ease.

Perhaps even allure.

Δὲν ἔχει τίποτα νὰ πεῖ.
Πιάνεται μόνο
καὶ κοιτάζεται
καὶ θέλει

She has nothing to say.
She simply touches herself
and watches herself
and wants

Ἐνῶ ὁλόκληρες φράσεις περνοῦν καὶ τὶς δέχεται
καὶ διατρέχει συνεχῶς μεγάλο κίνδυνο
ἀκόμα τὸ κορμὶ ποὺ θυμόταν
ἀλλὰ ὑπῆρχε κάτι ποὺ δὲν εἶχε ξαναδεῖ.

While whole phrases pass by and she accepts them
and she constantly faces great danger
still the body she remembered
but there was something she had never seen.

Ὡραῖα· κι ἂς εἶναι θλιβερὸ
γιατὶ δὲν παύει νά 'ναι ὡς τὰ σήμερα
νὰ σκύβει πάνω ἀπ' τὸ κορμί της
καὶ ν' ἀνασαίνει μὲ φωνές.

Ἔπειτα εἶναι μόνη της·
δὲν ἐμπιστεύεται κανέναν ὅταν λέει
χαϊδεύω τὸ κορμί μου
χαϊδεύω τὸ ἀδέξιο σῶμα μου.

Ὄχι πὼς ἔχει σημασία·
λίγο τὴ νοιάζει
γιατὶ χρυσὸ ἐλάφι στὴν κοιλάδα
ὀνειρευόταν νὰ ξαπλώνει.

Fine; even if sad
since until now it has never ceased being
leaning over her body
and breathing with voices.

Then she is alone;
she trusts no one when she says
I caress my body
I caress my awkward body.

Not that it matters;
she hardly minds
because she dreamt herself lying down
a golden deer in the valley.

2

Δὲν ὑπάρχει καμιὰ ἀμφιβολία.
Καὶ ἡ κατεύθυνση
καὶ ὁ προορισμὸς
(μετωπικὸς κι ἀφύσικος)
τὸ μαρτυροῦν.
Λίθινο βέβαια
ἀναθηματικό.

There is no doubt.
Both the orientation
and the inclination
(frontal and unnatural)
prove it.
Stone, of course
anathematic.

Ὅταν ἄρχισε νὰ θυμᾶται
ἦταν καλοκαίρι
δὲν ὑπῆρχε ἄλλος
κι ἔπαιρνε μόνο ὅ,τι ἤθελε.

When she began to remember
it was summer;
no one else existed
and she took only what she wanted.

Στρώνει ἕνα κρεβάτι ἄδειο
ἥσυχα μελετάει τὴν ἀπόφασή της
μέσα στὸ φῶς.

She makes an empty bed;
calmly she contemplates her decision
in the light.

Ἐπειδὴ ἀπόψε
περνοῦσε μὲ ἄμαξα μπροστὰ στὸ καλοκαίρι
κι ἔνιωθε τὴν ἀνάγκη νὰ ξεχάσει
ὅτι στὰ ὄνειρά της ἦταν πάντα ἕνα δέντρο
ἕνα ἀπ' τὰ πολλὰ
γεμάτη δάκρυα
καὶ τώρα ἐπιστρέφει.

Because tonight
she passed before summer in a coach
and felt the need to forget
that in her dreams she was always a tree
one in many
full of tears
and now she returns.

Μὲ ῥὸζ ὀμπρέλα κάποτε
διέσχιζε τὸν ψίθυρο καὶ τὴ σιωπὴ

Once with a pink umbrella
she walked across the whispers and silence

Ἡ Μαρία μπροστά της
μὲ βουτηγμένο τὸ κορμὶ ὥς τὴ μέση.
Ἄν ἀποφάσιζε νὰ μείνει ἢ νὰ φύγει
ἦταν ἐκεῖ.

Maria in front of her
in up to her waist.
Whether she decided to stay or leave
she was there.

Ἕνας ὑπαινιγμὸς γιὰ κείνη
θὰ καταλήξει στὴ μελαγχολία
ὄχι γιατὶ θὰ πέφτει μαλακὰ τὸ βράδυ
ἀλλὰ γιατὶ πληγώνεται γιὰ χάρη της ἀκόμα.

Βγαίνοντας ἀπὸ τὴν πλαγιὰ στὸ δρόμο
προσπάθησε νὰ μὴν προσέχει τὴ σιωπή.

A hint of her
will end in melancholy
not because night will fall softly
but because she is still in pain for her sake.

Coming off the verge onto the road
she tried not to notice the silence.

Χαμογελάει τὶς περισσότερες φορές.
Αὐτὴ ἡ Μαρία
ἀπὸ τὴν ἄποψη αὐτὴ—

Most times she smiles.
This Maria
from this perspective—

3

Δὲν μπορεῖ νὰ ἀποδοθεῖ σὲ κανέναν
κι αὐτὸ τὸ ξέρει ἄθελά της.

She cannot be attributed to anyone
and she knows it unwittingly.

Εἶχε μπλεχτεῖ στὸ νόημα
μιᾶς ἄκαιρης λέξης
—τί σημασία ἔχει πιά;
Ὅταν γεμάτη φόβο καὶ λύπη
γύρισε νὰ κοιτάξει τοὺς ἄλλους
ἡ λέξη μεγάλωσε.

She had become tangled in the meaning
of an untimely word
—what does it matter now?
When full of fear and sadness
she turned to look at the others
the word grew larger.

Κάθεται, κι ἀνάμεσα σ' αὐτὴν δὲν ὑπάρχει
πρώτη φορὰ δὲν ὑπάρχει·
γιὰ ποιὸ λόγο πρέπει ν' ἀπαντήσει;

Θυμᾶμαι εἶπε κάτι γιὰ τ' ἀπόγευμα
κι ἔμεινε στὴν κατάσταση αὐτὴ
χωρὶς ν' ἀλλάξει θέση.

She sits, and between her she does not exist
for the first time she does not exist;
why should she answer?

I remember she said something about the afternoon
and remained in that state
without changing positions.

Πίνει ἔνα φλιτζάνι τσάι
καὶ χαίρεται
νὰ ἀνάβει ἔνα τσιγάρο.
Δὲ θὰ γεράσει ἥσυχα.

She drinks a cup of tea
and gets pleasure
from lighting a cigarette.
She will not grow old calmly.

Νὰ ζεῖ
ν᾽ ἀπολαμβάνει μιὰ γεμάτη μέρα
νὰ κλείνει τὸ παράθυρο, ἀλλιῶς
τί ἄξιζαν οἱ μαγικές της ἱκανότητες.

To live
to enjoy a full day
to close the window, otherwise
what was her magic worth?

Στέκεται μὲ τὴν πλάτη στὸ παράθυρο·
τὸ βάζο
ἡ πρόθεση τῶν λουλουδιῶν.
Λέει στὸν ἀμαξὰ νὰ περιμένει.

She stands with her back to the window;
the vase
the intention of flowers.
She tells the coachman to wait.

Τὸ φῶς καὶ ἡ σκιὰ θὰ ἀντιγράφονται
χωρὶς καμία ἔμπνευση
μὲ ἀποτέλεσμα νὰ γίνει ἀφηρημένη·
ἄ, ἐπιτέλους, θά 'βλεπε τὸ τέλος.

The light and shade will be copied
without any inspiration
so that she becomes abstract;
ah, at last, she would see the end.

νὰ φορέσει τὰ ροῦχα της
νὰ χτενίσει τὰ μαλλιά της
νὰ βγεῖ στὸ δρόμο
νὰ περάσει ἀπέναντι

to wear her clothes
to comb her hair
to go out on the street
to cross over

Ἦρθε κοντά του τρέμοντας
ώσπου φτάνει, φτάνει
κι ἂς πεθάνει καθένας μόνος του.

She came close to him trembling
until enough, enough
just let each of us die alone.

Τρία ὁλόκληρα λεπτὰ προτοῦ οὐρλιάξει—
Καθισμένη στὸ κίτρινο φῶς
ἑνὸς προχωρημένου ἀπογεύματος
οἱ θάμνοι χρυσοὶ
ὅ,τι δὲν ἀγαποῦσε ἔλειπε
ἔμειν᾽ ἐκεῖ ἀκίνητη
τρία ὁλόκληρα λεπτὰ προτοῦ οὐρλιάξει.

Ὅταν τὴν ταρακούνησαν ἀπάντησε:
Τὴν ἑπόμενη φορὰ
θὰ μποροῦσα νὰ μιλήσω μὲ κάποιον
καὶ ν᾽ ἀγαπήσω, ἂν χρειαστεῖ.

Three whole minutes before she howled—
Seated in the yellow light
of an advancing afternoon
the bushes were golden
what she did not love was missing
she stayed there motionless
three whole minutes before she howled.
When they shook her she replied:
Next time
I will be able to talk with someone
and to love, if necessary.

4

Εἶχε ξεχάσει·
οἱ ἄλλοι ὅλοι θὰ κοιμοῦνται
ἐνῶ αὐτὴ
τρελὰ λόγια ψιθυρίζει στὸν καθρέφτη της.

She had forgotten;
the others will be sleeping
while she
whispers crazy words in her mirror.

Λοιπὸν
ἡ Μαρία
ὅταν κανεὶς δὲν τὴν προσέχει
ταχτοποιεῖ τὰ χέρια της.

So
Maria
when no one is watching her
arranges her hands.

Δὲ θέλει ἀκόμα νὰ γυρίσει·
σηκώθηκε ἀπλῶς γιατὶ εἶναι τόσο ὄμορφα
κι οἱ μέρες μεγαλώνουν.

She does not want to return yet;
she got up simply because it's so beautiful
and the days grow longer.

Τὴν πῆγαν εὔκολα στὸ αὐτοκίνητο
καὶ βγαίνοντας ἀπὸ τὴν πόλη ἤξερε
ὅτι θὰ πάρει τὴ μορφὴ
ποὺ τώρα ἔχει γιὰ πάντα.
Ἀνοίγει λοιπὸν τὴ βεντάλια της.

They got her into the car easily
and as she left the city she knew
that she would take the shape
she now has forever.
So she unfolds her fan.

Εἶναι πολὺ εὐτυχισμένη ἐδῶ
κάθεται καὶ κοιτάζει καὶ
ὅταν ὁ ἥλιος παίρνει τὸ δωμάτιο
βλέπει καλὰ τὶς ὧρες νὰ περνοῦν.

Δὲ συμμετέχει
διαβάζω ὅμως καὶ
κοιμᾶμαι ἥσυχα τὰ βράδια.

Σκέφτομαι, καμιὰ φορὰ πετύχαινα γραμμὲς
σχεδὸν μὲ μονοκοντυλιά.

She is very happy here
she sits and stares
when the sun fills the room
she watches closely the hours passing.
She does not participate
I read, however, and
sleep calmly at night.
I think, sometimes I managed lines
in one pencil stroke.

Ξάπλωνε μὲ τὰ μάτια ἀνοιχτὰ
κανένας δὲν κατάλαβε ὅτι δὲν ἤτανε αὐτή.

She lay down with her eyes wide open
no one understood that it was not her.

5

Δὲν ἔκρυβε τὴν ἔκπληξή της.
Σ' ὅλη της τὴ ζωὴ ἦταν εὐτυχισμένη·
γιατὶ ἂν θέλησε νὰ βρεῖ δικαιολογίες
δὲν εἶχε καμιά.

She did not hide her surprise.
All through her life she was happy;
because if she wanted to find excuses
she had none.

Παρέσυρε μαζί της
καὶ τὰ πουλιά ἀπ' τὸ χαλὶ
κι ὕστερα βγῆκε
χωρὶς ἀγκῶνες
χωρὶς γόνατα.

She even dragged with her
the birds from the rug
and then she left
without elbows
or knees.

Ἐκεῖ, ψιθύρισε
ἐκεῖ τὴν ἔβλεπα τὴ θάλασσα.

There, she whispered
there, I could see the sea.

Ἀπὸ τὴν πρώτη κιόλας ἐπαφὴ
δὲν παρουσίασε ἀντίσταση·
ὁλόκληρο τὸ κορμί της εὐφραινόταν.
Παρέδωσε λοιπὸν στὶς στάχτες
ὅ,τι ἀπόμενε ὀρθὸ
κάηκαν ὅλα, τότε.
Τὴν ἴδια μοίρα γνώρισε
κι ὁ πρωινὸς περίπατος.

From the very first touch
she did not resist;
her whole body rejoiced.
She consigned to the ashes
whatever was left
everything burned, then.
Even the morning stroll
came to a similar fate.

Φόρεσε τὸ κασκόλ της
ἔσβησε τὸ φῶς
ἐδῶ καὶ ἕξι νύχτες πεθαμένη
προσέχοντας μὴν ξεχαστεῖ
σὲ κάτι τόσο εὔθραυστο
βγῆκε στὸ δρόμο
καὶ μπροστὰ στὰ μάτια της
τὴν τίναξε
πρὶν ἀπὸ πόσα χρόνια τώρα
ὁ πρωινὸς ἀέρας.

She put on her scarf
turned off the light
dead for six nights now
careful not to lose herself
in something so fragile
she went out into the street
and in front of her eyes
how many years ago now?
the morning wind
jolted her.

Δὲν εἶχε σκοτεινιάσει ἀκόμα
κι ἴσως πραγματικὰ νὰ ἦταν
μέσα στὰ σάλια καὶ τὸ γέλιο της
ἀνόητη, ἀλλὰ
δὲν εἶχε σκοτεινιάσει ἀκόμα
ὅταν ἕνα βαθὺ φτερὸ
πέρασε ἀπ' τὰ μάτια της
ἕνα μελίσσι μὲ φωνές.

It had not gotten dark yet
and perhaps she really was
in all her spittle and laughter
a fool, but
it had not gotten dark yet
when a deep wing
passed before her eyes
a swarm with voices.

Τὸ ἀπόγευμα
ἐνῶ ἡ πόλη ἦταν χαμηλὰ
ἡ Μαρία κατέλαβε ὁλόκληρο τὸ σῶμα της.

In the afternoon
while the city was down low
Maria took over her whole body.

6

Στὴ μέση ἑνὸς ἔξοχου κύκλου
ἀπὸ μεστὰ νοήματα
ἡ Μαρία στάθηκε
καὶ βγῆκε στὴ φωτογραφία
σιγανὰ
φτιάχνοντας τὴ φουρκέτα στὰ μαλλιὰ της.

Ἐκθαμβωτικὸς ἀέρας
φυσοῦσε τὴν ἀδιαφορία της.

In the middle of an exquisite circle
ripe with meaning
Maria stood
and appeared in the photograph
slowly
fixing the pin in her hair.

A dazzling wind
blew at her indifference.

Γδύθηκε στὸ σκοτάδι
πλάι στὰ φλιτζανάκια τοῦ καφὲ
καὶ τὸ καλὸ τραπεζομάντιλο.

Ἐντελῶς ἄλλα λόγια σκεφτόταν.

She undressed in the dark
next to the coffee cups
and the best tablecloth.

She was thinking completely different words.

Σχεδίασε μὲ τὴ φωνή της ἔνα ψέμα·
ἡ Μαρία στὸν χλιαρὸ ἥλιο
σὲ βάζα ἀπὸ σμάλτο
ψιθυριστά.

She made up a lie with her voice;
Maria in the tepid sun
in vases of enamel
whispering.

Χρησιμοποίησε τὴ μέρα της ἁπλὰ
καὶ δὲ χρησίμευε σὲ τίποτα

She used her day simply
and she was of no use

Κρατοῦσε σοβαρὴ τὸ σῶμα της
στὸ χόλ, στὸ δρόμο
ἀνάμεσα σὲ ἄλλους.
Ἔβλεπε πράγματα νὰ μεγαλώνουν·
μήπως μιὰ ἄλλη ποὺ κοιτάζει ἔξω;

Ἐκεῖ ἔξω
ἔξω ἀπ' τὸ ἄσπρο της πρόσωπο
δυνάμωσε χωρὶς νὰ προσέξει
ὅτι γινόταν ὄμορφη.

Serious, she held her body
in the hall, in the street
in the midst of others.
She saw things grow;
could it be someone else staring out?

Out there
outside her white face
she grew strong without noticing
that she was becoming beautiful.

Ἀπὸ τὴ μιὰ στιγμὴ στὴν ἄλλη
ἔπεφτε ἔξω καὶ τῆς ἄρεσε
ἀλλὰ αὐτὸ δὲν τὴν ἀπασχολοῦσε τώρα πιὰ
ἂν καὶ παρέμεινε εὐδιάκριτη
νὰ ἀπαντάει καὶ νὰ ἔρχεται.

Μήπως μιὰ ἄλλη ποὺ κοιτάζει ἔξω;

From one minute to the next
she fell out of line and liked it
but this no longer concerned her
though she could still be seen
answering and approaching.

Could it be someone else staring out?

Ἔπεσε ἀπ' τὸ σῶμα της
κύλησε μαλακὰ πάνω στὸ χιόνι
ἀπὸ μέρα σὲ μέρα·
ἴσως ὑπάρχει ἕνα τέτοιο μέρος, σκέφτηκε
ἀλλὰ παλιὸ καὶ ἥσυχο
καθόλου πειρασμὸς
καθόλου ἔρωτας.

Χαμήλωσε λοιπὸν τὴ βεντάλια της.

She fell out of her body
and rolled softly on top of the snow
from day to day;
perhaps a place like this exists, she thought
but old and quiet
no temptation
no love.
So she lowered her fan.

7

Ἡ Μαρία πέρασε καὶ κάθισε
ἔστρωσε ἥσυχα τὸ φόρεμά της
χωρὶς ν' ἀγαπάει
χωρὶς τὴν ἔξαψη νὰ πληγωθεῖ
περιεργάστηκε τὶς ἐποχὲς στὸ χιόνι
κι ἔδιωξε ἁπαλὰ τὴ μνήμη ἀπὸ τὸ στόμα της.

Κάθε λίγα βήματα
προχωροῦσε τὸ σούρουπο.

Maria came in and sat down
she slowly straightened her dress
without loving
without the heat of being hurt
she contemplated the seasons in the snow
and gently chased the memory from her mouth.

Every few steps
dusk advanced.

Φτιάχνει ἕναν κύκλο
ἕνα μικρότερο
ἕναν ἀκόμα πιὸ μικρό.

Οὔτε μιὰ φορὰ ἀπὸ τότε
δὲ θά 'ναι ἐκεῖ ν' ἀκούσει.
Τί; εἶπε
πρὶν προχωρήσει στὸ ποτάμι.

She makes a circle
a smaller one
an even smaller one.

She won't be there to hear
not once since then.
What? she said
before she stepped into the river.

ἄλλωστε στὴν ἀφήγηση αὐτὴ
φαίνεται ἡ ἀδυναμία
νὰ βρεθεῖ ἕνας χῶρος

besides in this narrative
the difficulty
of finding a space is clear

Ἡ Μαρία μόνη της
ἀκουμπισμένη σὲ θαμπὴ βροχὴ
οἱ φούξιες φορτωμένες ἄνθη.
Τὸ τελευταῖο πράγμα ποὺ συγκράτησε
πιὸ χαμηλὰ
λιγάκι δεξιότερα...

Maria alone
leaning on turbid rain
the fuchsias loaded with blossoms.
The last thing she remembered
a little lower
a little to the right...

Ἔσκυβε νὰ σηκώσει τὴ ζακέτα της
μὲ φόντο ἄλλοτε τὸ δάσος
κι ἄλλοτε τὶς καρέκλες στὴν παλιά τους θέση.

Παρμένη ὅμως ἀπὸ χαμηλὰ
καὶ μ᾽ ἕναν ἀκαθόριστο ἀέρα.

Τοὺς δυὸ αἰῶνες ποὺ ἀκολούθησαν
ἀγνόησε τὸ μέταλλο καὶ τὸ μπαμπάκι
κι ἁπλώθηκε νοτιοανατολικά.

She was leaning over to pick up her jacket
sometimes against a forest background
sometimes with the chairs in their old position.
Taken however from below
and with an undefined air.
In the two centuries that followed
she ignored metal and cotton
and spread out southeastward.

8

Παρ' ὅτι δὲν ἐξιχνιάζει τίποτα
πλημμύριζε τὰ πεζοδρόμια
καὶ φύτρωνε

Even though she solves nothing
she flooded the sidewalks
and sprouted

Στὴν καλύτερη μορφή της
παρέμεινε ἀτάραχη
ἐνῶ τὸ σῶμα ἔγερνε μὲ μιὰ χαριτωμένη κίνηση

Toward her most perfect form
she remained untroubled
while her body bent with a charming dip

Ἕνα παιχνίδι τοῦ φωτὸς
ὅπως ὅλοι μας τέλος πάντων

A game of light
like all of us after all

Δὲ σκέφτεται νὰ δεῖ κανέναν·
μάλιστα τὶς περισσότερες φορὲς
ὁ ἔρωτάς της ἦταν ἄτυχος

She does not think of seeing anyone;
besides most of the time
her love failed

Θὰ κάθεται λοιπὸν
ἢ εἶναι ξαπλωμένη

So she may be sitting
or she is lying down

Πολὺ ἀργότερα
πέρασε ἕνα βαθυγάλαζο λιοντάρι
κι ἐκείνη φόρεσε τὸ σάλι της

Much later
a deep blue lion passed
and she put on her shawl

Ἐπικαλέστηκε τὸ ὄνομά της
κι ἀνασηκώθηκε σὲ ἄλλη ἐποχή.

She invoked her name
and was lifted into another era.

Ἐπίλογος

Epilogue

Εἶμαι στὴν ἀρχὴ τῆς ζωῆς μου καὶ εἶμαι ἔξω στὸ φῶς. Ἔχουν περάσει χρόνια ἀπὸ τότε καὶ προσπαθῶ νὰ ρουφήξω τὸ ἄσπρο. Μόνο τὸ φῶς χρειαζόμουν. Ὕστερα, σκέφτηκα, θὰ σταματήσω νὰ κάνω αὐτὸν τὸ θόρυβο. Ἂν σταματήσω νὰ κάνω αὐτὸν τὸ θόρυβο, θ' ἀκούσω κάτι πολὺ ὄμορφο. Δὲν ξέρω ἀκόμα, ἀλλὰ εἶμαι σίγουρη, κι αὐτὸ μοῦ συμβαίνει συχνά. Μοῦ συμβαίνει συχνὰ ἐκεῖ ποὺ κάθομαι καὶ σκέφτομαι, ἀλλὰ δὲν εἶναι καθόλου αὐτό. Καθόλου κάτι ποὺ σκέφτομαι, ἀλλ' αὐτὸ μὲ βοηθάει. Μὲ βοηθάει νὰ μὴν ἔχω τὸ νοῦ μου, νὰ μὴν περιμένω τίποτα. Γιατὶ τότε τίποτα δὲ θὰ μποροῦσε νὰ συμβεῖ, ἐκτὸς ἀπὸ κάτι ποὺ ἤδη τὸ ξέρω. Καὶ τί ξέρω ἐγώ; Τί ξέρω;

I am at the beginning of my life and I am out in the light. Many years have passed since then and I am trying to suck in the white. I only needed light. Later, I thought, I will stop making that noise. If I stop making that noise, I will hear something very beautiful. I do not know yet, but I am certain, and that happens to me often. It happens to me often when I sit and think, but it is not at all that. Not at all something I think, but it helps. It helps if my mind is elsewhere, if I am not waiting for anything. Because then nothing can happen, except for something I already know. And me, what do I know? What do I know?

Notes to the poems

◊ *p. 23* ◊ The description refers to the Minoan frescoes of women and dolphins found in the Knossos Palace in Crete.

◊ *p. 27* ◊ The reference to women turning into trees is a mainstay of classical literature; the particular case of a woman turning into a birch can be found in both Sappho and Ovid.

◊ *p. 29* ◊ "The past scrubbed with water and ashes" refers to the way women in Greece would wash white fabric with ash.

◊ *p. 33* ◊ The last line is taken from a Greek translation of Shakespeare's *King Lear* where Lear is struggling with madness and asks, "Where have I been? Where am I? Fair daylight?"

◊ *p. 35* ◊ The reference to the two triangles and the color yellow recalls the paintings of Joan Miró. See "The Hunter (Catalan Landscape)."

◊ *p. 41* ◊ The line translated, "the body she remembered," could also be rendered, "the body that remembered."

◊ *p. 47* ◊ The archaeological term "anathematic" refers to a votive offering or dedication carved in marble.

◊ *p. 75* ◊ The Greek word πρόθεση means both "preposition" and "intention."

◊ *p. 125* ◊ In the Greek edition the italicized line *"could it be someone else staring out?"* is mirrored on the right-hand page in the line from the next poem "Could it be someone else staring out?" creating the illusion that the page itself is a mirror.

◊ *p. 135* ◊ This refers to the writer Virginia Woolf who committed suicide by drowning.

◊ *p. 155* ◊ See Henri Rousseau's "The Sleeping Gypsy."

◊ *p. 157* ◊ In Greek the same verb form ἐπικαλέστηκε is used for both the reflexive and middle senses. "She invoked her name" could also be translated, "Her name was invoked."

About the Author

Born in 1947 in Patras, Maria Laina is widely regarded as one of Greece's most important living poets. Her work includes nine poetry collections, eleven plays, five books of prose, four critical studies, and an anthology of twentieth-century poetry in Greek translations. She is the recipient of several awards, including the Greek National Prize for Poetry (1994), the Maria Callas Award (1998), the Cavafy Award (2006), and the Athens Academy Prize (2015) for her book of collected poems (1970-2012). A recent collection, Ό,τι έγινε: Άνθρωποι και φαντάσματα (*Whatever Happened: People and Ghosts*), received the Reader's Prize in 2021.

About the Translator

Karen Van Dyck's books include *Kassandra and the Censors, The Rehearsal of Misunderstanding, The Scattered Papers of Penelope, Austerity Measures: The New Greek Poetry*, and the co-edited Norton anthology, *The Greek Poets: Homer to the Present*. Her essays, translations, and poetry have appeared in *The Paris Review, The Guardian, LARB, Ποιητική (Poiitiki)*, and *Tender*. She is founding director of Hellenic Studies in the Classics Department at Columbia University, where she teaches courses on translation, gender, and Modern Greek literature.

The text of *Hers* is set in
Cormorant Garamond (English)
and Garamond Premier Pro (Greek).
Typesetting by Ainee Jeong and Don't Look Now.
Cover design by Dalia Karpaviciute.
Printed and bound in Saline, Michigan
at McNaughton & Gunn.